# Guide to Supporting Children through Bereavement and Loss

Currently, many children are unable to access emotional support services, and other members of a child's support network are required to provide this emotional guidance and support. This resource book has been written to support children when they have experienced a loss or bereavement. It is intended to be used as a guide by families and friends, school staff, and all other adults supporting children through their grief, to help them to provide this emotional guidance.

*Guide to Supporting Children through Bereavement and Loss* offers information, education, and guidance about how to understand grief, ways to support the process and emotions of grief, and to help children to express themselves and make sense of their changed world. It covers the 'stages of grief', and holds many practical ideas and activities designed to help children to process and understand their grief, as well as to express and explore their emotions. There is a section on undertaking group work for bereaved children, as well as information on both self-care and what to do when a referral to a specialist service may be required.

This guide was designed to be used by any person supporting a child through loss or bereavement, no matter what their previous understanding of these issues. It is specifically written to be as accessible and as user-friendly as possible to help, rather than hinder, the user. It can be used alone, or alongside the storybook *When the Sun Fell Out of the Sky*.

**Hollie Rankin** is a counsellor who has worked with and supported children, young people and their families within schools in the North East over the last ten years. Her recent books on trauma and bereavement were prompted by a noticeable gap in resources to help to guide adults when supporting children in emotionally challenging circumstances.

# Guide to Supporting Children through Bereavement and Loss

## Emotional Wellbeing in School and at Home

HOLLIE RANKIN

Routledge
Taylor & Francis Group

LONDON AND NEW YORK

First published 2019
by Routledge
2 Park Square, Milton Park, Abingdon, Oxon OX14 4RN

and by Routledge
52 Vanderbilt Avenue, New York, NY 10017

*Routledge is an imprint of the Taylor & Francis Group, an informa business*

*British Library Cataloguing-in-Publication Data*
A catalogue record for this book is available from the British Library

*Library of Congress Cataloging-in-Publication Data*
Names: Rankin, Hollie, author.
Title: Guide to supporting children through bereavement and loss : emotional wellbeing in school
    and at home / Hollie Rankin.
Description: Abingdon, Oxon ; New York, NY : Routledge, 2019. I Includes bibliographical references.
Identifiers: LCCN 2018057110 I ISBN 9781138360419 (pbk) I ISBN 9780429433160 (ebk)
Subjects: LCSH: Bereavement in children. I Loss (Psychology) in children. I Grief in children. I
    Children—Counseling of. I School mental health services. I Students—Mental health services.
Classification: LCC BF723 .G75 R365 2019 I DDC 155.9/37083—dc23
LC record available at https://lccn.loc.gov/2018057110

ISBN: 978-1-138-36041-9 (pbk)
ISBN: 978-0-429-43316-0 (ebk)

Typeset in Antitled
by Apex CoVantage, LLC

I would like to thank everyone who has helped in the creation of this book; for everything from positive thoughts to sharing opinions, from proofreading and healing to new stationery and patience, from laughs and sarcasm to childcare and time, and for telling me I could when I thought I couldn't, thank you.

To my four parents, I love you all.

I would like to dedicate this book to all of the children I know, and have known, who have experienced the devastating loss of a loved one.

# Contents

# Introduction

There can often be anxiety that working with emotion means years and years of training and certificates. There is some truth in this, and, as a qualified counsellor myself, I am a great believer that this is to some extent desirable. However, I have also worked alongside some of the most capable, caring, empathic and dedicated people who are not officially 'qualified', but who, nonetheless, are often more than qualified in so many other ways to support children. They bring with them their wealth of knowledge, their experience of relationships with children and families, their own personal and professional experiences, and, above all else, an absolute dedication to supporting children.

I strongly believe that every school should have access to their own counsellor or counselling service. However, being realistic, we have to note that schools are running out of money to pay for such services. This means that more and more teachers and teaching assistants are providing daily emotional support for more and more children. It is what it is, and, although deeply regrettable, we have to do our very best to fill these financial holes with emotional support.

Due to the lack of outside agencies to support children, it is also falling to parents, family members, foster carers, support and social workers to take on an even greater role in helping children explore and manage their emotions.

This book was written to help provide some guidance and ideas for the people who tirelessly support children in schools, communities and at home, in order to help them to find their way again.

> If you want to go quickly, go alone. If you want to go far, go together.
> African proverb

# Considerations

Please bear in mind that not all activities are suited to every child, they may need to be changed or adapted to suit each child's level of understanding and their individual journey. Children need information to be shared with them using appropriate language for their level of understanding.

Some of the exercises ask that the child closes their eyes, to help reduce sensory distractions, and to help the child to focus on what they can hear. There could be many different reasons why a child might not wish to do this, and we need to respect their decision.

It is important to ensure that it is possible for children to take some extra time to process their emotions after completing activities, so that they are not left in a vulnerable or distressed state.

When supporting children, you may need to consider an onward referral to a mental health service. It can be helpful to know your local referral system and how to access other services, particularly when children need to receive in-depth one-to-one support.

# 1. Grief

## How do I talk to a child about death?

This can be one of the most difficult and challenging conversations you may ever have. Keeping these few guidelines in mind may be helpful. Be honest above all else. Explain things as honestly as possible, taking into account the child's level of understanding, while using appropriate language. Avoid using metaphors, which may confuse the child, complicate things or scare them.

- Talk to the child as soon as possible after the death.
- Break information down into smaller pieces, so as not to overload the child.
- Avoid using words like 'asleep', 'lost' or 'gone away'.
- Not knowing can often be worse than knowing – children will often fill in the blanks with all sorts of information they have imagined.

If the child asks you something you don't know the answer to, be honest and say you don't know, but will try to find out. You don't have to know all the answers, and children will appreciate you being honest, rather than trying to change the subject or making something up. Children often know instinctively when we aren't being truthful.

Children might laugh or refuse to believe what you are telling them, which is their brain's defence mechanism as they process this information. Children may also act aloof or ask questions that might seem completely inappropriate or uncaring, such as 'Does that mean we don't have to visit the hospital any more?', or 'Can I have his Lego?'. Again, this is them processing information and does not mean that they do not care.

## The impact of grief

Grief is a normal human response to loss, however the journey that each person takes through their grief is hugely individual. Bereavement can affect children and adults in many ways, and it may impact behaviour and mood in lots of different ways. Children are likely to experience a huge range of emotions when they are bereaved, as well as the bereavement affecting their behaviour, mood, sleep patterns and eating habits. There is no way to predict how a child will respond to grief, but there is certain information that can be useful to bear in mind.

When children are bereaved, they not only mourn the loss of the person, but also the changes that the death brings to their world. This can include the loss of their 'normal' life and routines, of attention or comfort, of confidence in themselves or in others, and of the world around them, as well as the loss of security, stability and safety.

For children it can be particularly scary to experience the loss of the living as well as the person who died. This can happen when the people around the child are unable to give them the emotional support they need because they themselves are, understandably, consumed by grief.

Children can become 'clingy' to adults around them, at home or at school, and are likely to need more comfort and time. Some children become withdrawn and quiet, whereas others may become angry and aggressive. Children can worry that they somehow caused the death, that they themselves might die, or that their remaining family members may die – and then who will look after them?

Even if they don't directly share these worries, it might be worth considering talking through them, in case these are concerns that the child has.

Children will often act out their feelings rather than talk about them. Even adults struggle with trying to explain grief in words, so it is little wonder that children do. Children communicate through behaviour, and it is our job as adults to notice what they are telling us by how they are acting.

Due to children's emotional development, it is likely that they will be distracted from their grief for periods of time – they may be unable to focus on their grief in the same way an adult might. They may jump in and out of their sadness and grief and we need to remember that they do not have to focus on their grief at all points in time. This helps to protect them emotionally and mentally, even though it might appear odd to adults: it does not mean the child does not care, it is a normal response and should be treated as such.

When children are bereaved it is usual that they will revisit their grief at each developmental stage throughout their life, processing emotions and experiences from a different perspective. They may wonder what life could have been like if they had not lost someone they dearly loved, grieving for what could have been had the person lived.

We cannot protect and shelter children from grief; unfortunately it is a result of loving someone dearly. However, we can help children as they navigate through their grief and support them along the way. We can try to hold their hearts, as well as their hands, on this difficult journey.

> It has helped to have some ideas about how to get the kids to talk about their Dad and their feelings and grief. I don't feel so lost, or worried that they are avoiding things any more.
> Foster carer supporting children with loss

# How grief can present

This is famously outlined as the 'five stages of grief'. People move through these stages, not always in a strict or logical order, and often revisit different stages many times. People spend varied amounts of time working through each stage, and it is important to remember that everyone has their own experience of grief and there is no right or wrong. The five stages can be helpful to bear in mind when supporting a bereaved child, and may help you to gain an understanding of where they may be emotionally.

*Denial* – Denial can often be a form of temporary defence, thoughts such as 'This isn't happening' or 'It can't be real'. Feelings often include fear, numbness, shock and confusion.

*Anger* – During this stage anger can often be misdirected or misplaced. Feelings of envy and rage can make it difficult to support people during this stage. Feelings can include anxiety, irritation, guilt, blame and frustration.

*Bargaining* – This stage involves the hope that, through bargaining within their mind or maybe with a higher power, reality can be changed in some way. Thoughts such as 'I will give anything to bring them back'. People can often feel compelled to tell their story, and can be left feeling a sense of desperation, intense loss and helplessness.

*Depression* – This is an important part of grieving and a time when people realise that their loss is real. Feelings often include helplessness, intense sadness, hopelessness and lack of energy.

*Acceptance* – A sense that life can go on after the death, some level of adjustment to life without the person, and some level of acceptance of their loss.

Kubler-Ross, E. (1975) *Death*. New York: Simon & Schuster

Grief can often manifest itself as a physical pain, particularly in children, and they may experience symptoms such as headaches, muscle aches, fatigue, exhaustion, chest pain or tightness and stomach pains, to name a few.

My legs hurt, my tummy hurts, and my head hurts … it all just hurts.
6-year-old boy whose Mum suddenly passed away

# What do bereaved children need?

After bereavement we can be left feeling helpless, and powerless to make things better for others. We often don't know how to act, or what to do or say. These are normal reactions to have when supporting bereaved people.

There *are* certain things we can do, and put in place, in order to support bereaved children, however. Please note that these are not in any particular order and also that there may be more than you feel are necessary, but this list is intended to give you a range of options to choose from. Bereaved children need to:

• Experience acceptance and empathy.
• Be supported to understand their emotions.
• Grieve at their own pace.
• Be encouraged to express their thoughts and emotions.

- Be listened to.
- Be able to ask questions.
- Be helped to find some ways of managing.
- Understand the reality of what has happened.
- Be supported to adjust to life without the person who has died.
- Experience care, love, hugs, connection, patience, reassurance and understanding.
- Experience continuity – keep to established routines as much as possible.
- Experience good communication between home and school.
- Have opportunities to remember the person who died.
- Have a key person/people both at home and at school.
- Tell their story and feel heard. Sharing their story can help children to heal; they might need to tell this over and over.

## How can we do this?

- Listen.
- Be there.
- Accept their emotions.
- Use open questions.
- Refer child to appropriate support when required.
- Don't try to dig too deep, respect what the child shares.
- Be reliable.
- Reassure the child that however they are feeling is normal and there are no right or wrong ways to feel.

# 2. Listening

If a child's feelings are ignored or denied they may learn not to trust their feelings, not to listen to them, or find they don't understand their meaning.

The following are some tips on how to help children to feel heard and listened to. The suggestions may also be helpful ways of encouraging children to share their thoughts and feelings more openly with you. I'm sure you will already have your own style, skills and ways of helping children to express themselves and share their thoughts and feelings, these are just some further suggestions:

- Spending time with the child, making sure you actually have the time to listen to them with your full attention, can be huge to a child, particularly when they live in a world where parents and families are often distracted, teachers are over-stretched, and their friends and siblings are often preoccupied. Children very quickly learn to spot the signs that someone is not really listening to them and will often give up trying. It can be difficult to find the time, but it can make all the difference in the world to the child.
- Side-by-side talking can be really effective for some children. This is when you are both taking part in an activity together and talking at the same time, often side-by-side. Examples of this are colouring-in, washing dishes, fishing, going for a walk, baking, driving in the car or gardening. For some children, the intensity of sitting opposite an adult, making eye-contact, and being expected to share thoughts and feelings, can feel too much. Side-by-side talking allows children to be engaged in an activity and this in itself may help them to feel more relaxed, at ease, and more able to talk openly without an adult staring intently at them.
- Letting a child know you are listening to them can be done very easily by using simple comments such as 'mm hmm', 'oh', 'yes', 'uh huh' or 'go on'. This can encourage the child to continue to share with you, feel that you are listening with genuine interest, and to feel that you understand what they are telling you. It can help to demonstrate empathy and acceptance of what they are saying. Children often don't need you to solve their problems – they just need to feel heard. When a child feels heard, they will often come to their own conclusion about how to move forward, but you could see if they would like to explore their options together.
- Some children struggle with naming their feelings, they may say things like 'I really wanted to punch him today'. Naming the feeling the child is expressing can help them to begin to make the link and build their emotional literacy. For example, a response may be 'It sounds like you were really ANGRY with him'. Again, this can demonstrate that you understand what the child is saying, and also how they are feeling.
- Try to avoid using the word 'why' when a child is sharing their thoughts and feelings with you. Often children can feel that 'why' is a judgement or an accusation. It can leave the child feeling ashamed or challenged, and stop them from continuing the conversation. Children sometimes don't know 'why' they did something or 'why' they feel the way they do. Using the phrase 'I wonder ...' can be useful in this situation. It is not a direct question, but more an invitation to respond if the child chooses to. Children may choose not to respond, and it

might appear that they have completely ignored you, but often they will look for an answer within their own mind, encouraging self-reflection.

When people listen to me talk about my Mum it makes me feel happy inside, because I can tell them all about her, so I don't forget her.
12-year-old girl

# 3. My first aid kit

Throughout this book are ideas, activities and tips for helping children to deal with their grief. There will naturally be some that children are more comfortable with than others, and some that they are more drawn towards. My hope is that you can help the child to fill up their own first aid kit, filled with activities or tips that they feel work for them; things that they might like to revisit at another time. The first aid kit can help children in a few ways. It can:

- Help children to remember there are things and people that can help.
- Empower children to help themselves.
- Remind children to access helpful activities when they need them.
- Help children to trust their own inner wisdom.
- Help to build children's self-confidence, self-esteem and resilience.

The first aid kit can be completed on paper: the child might like to create a poster or a pocket-sized first aid kit. It could also be a physical box, using an empty shoe or tissue box. Talk through the options with the child, it is to be *their* first aid kit, so helping them to take part in its creation is key. Suggest that they come up with a label for it that might mean something special to them. Encourage them to make the label and attach it to the box. It becomes theirs – a special box for special things.

There are many ideas that can be used in the approach to the first aid kit. The following are some suggestions for things that the child may wish to include:

- I can relax my mind by …
  Use the activities in this book to help the child to identify ways to relax their mind.

- I can relax my body by …
  Use the activities in this book to help the child to identify ways to relax their body.

- Who … who can I trust? Who is here to help me? At home, at school.
  Helping children to identify people around them who can support them can remind them that there are people they can rely on. The list could include friends, family, teachers, social or support workers, pets, or even soft toys – if the child feels they can be supported by them, they go on the list.

- If it is a first aid 'box', the child might wish to add pens, pencils and paper or some colouring sheets. Focusing on a simple activity such as colouring can help to relax the brain. Any colouring books or sheets can be used, or more intricate designs often known as 'mindful colouring' are available.

- Photographs, letters, memories, drawings or cards can be put in the first aid box or attached to a paper first aid kit.

- I feel good when …

  Help children to put together a list of activities or things that they find make them feel good or bring them comfort. Lists could include ideas such as: taking a hot-water bottle to bed, smelling my Mum's perfume, asking for a hug, stroking my dog, playing with my friends.

- I can move my body by …

  Help children create a list of physical activities that they enjoy, this could be a sport or activities such as doing 10 jumping jacks or 5 sit-ups.

- Children might like to include a tub of play dough or a fiddle toy/fidget toy in their first aid kit, something that can help to calm and release tension.

- A worry stone could be included – a smooth stone that can be held by the child and rubbed to help soothe them.

- Children might include a bottle of bubbles to help them with their 'bubble breathing' or they may keep a memory jar in their kit.

There is no end to the possibilities, and each child will create their own individual first aid kit. Get creative, open your mind, and go with it!

> I can use my first aid kit whenever I want to. I keep a copy at school and one at home too on my wall. My Dad knows when I am having a bad day too and he helps me choose something from my kit.
> 9-year-old girl whose Nan passed away

# First aid kit drawing

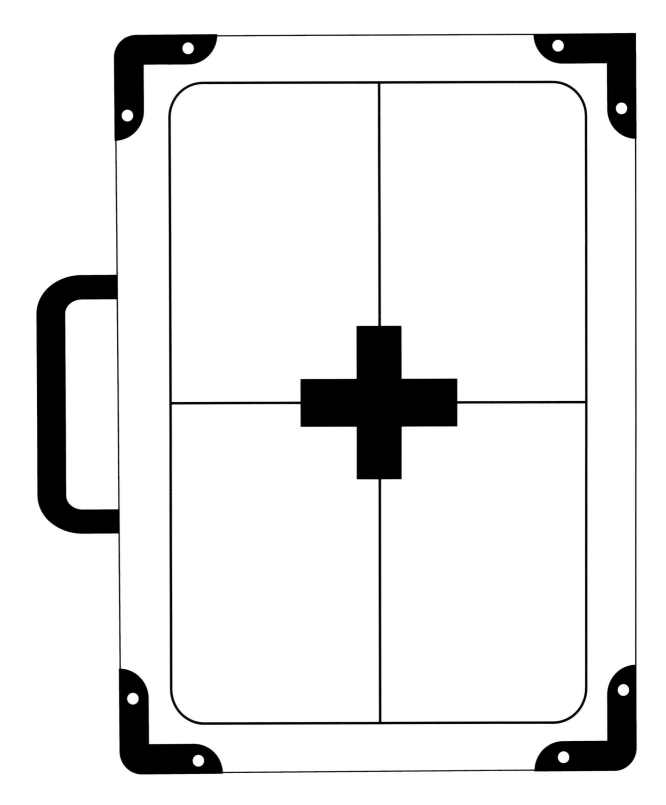

First aid kit drawing

# 4. Anxiety

It is natural for children to worry when they have experienced bereavement. Children may worry about how the person they loved died, if others around them will die, or if they themselves might become ill and die. Offering children a listening ear, support and reassurance, can help them to talk through these worries.

Sometimes children can experience anxiety as a result of loss. Children who may not have been anxious in the past may begin to feel anxious in situations that would not have fazed them previously. Anxiety is a normal emotion, but when it impacts on a child's ability to function in their everyday life, they may need some further support.

We can help children to understand anxiety, why people feel anxious, how anxiety can be useful – as well as when it is not – and how to overcome anxious thoughts and feelings.

Below is an example of how I usually explain anxiety to children. Please edit this however you like, and if you can fit it to match with the child's own life, then it will resonate even more with them.

Anxiety is designed to help keep us safe from danger. When we are scared or think something might hurt us, our body and brain react to help protect us. If you saw something was going to fall on you, you would probably either try to catch it, stop it, or get out of the way very quickly.

Thousands of years ago there were cavemen and women living on earth. They would go out hunting for food to eat. Imagine that, at the same time, there was a hungry sabre-toothed tiger looking for food too, and it has seen the tasty-looking caveman.

The caveman sees the danger and the 'worry alarm' inside him starts to work. When this happens, a certain part of the brain takes over. I call these parts the 'cave brain' (its real name is the amygdala) and the 'thinking brain' (the pre-frontal cortex).

The cave brain takes charge and sends signals to the body that say, to help the caveman survive, he needs to do one of three things: fight the animal (fight), run away (this is also called flight) or stay very still and hope he hasn't been spotted (freeze).

To do this, there are lots of changes in the body, which mean that we might feel:

- Sweaty or shaky.
- Our mouth becomes dry.
- Our muscles become tense and tight.

- Like we have butterflies in our tummy.
- Sick.
- Our heart beats faster.
- Our head begins to ache.
- We breathe faster and more heavily.

Nowadays there are no sabre-toothed tigers, but our brain can sometimes think that there is danger when there really isn't any. When this happens, the brain can set off a false alarm. This is a bit like when a smoke alarm goes off in the house when there isn't a fire; just a piece of toast that has been overcooked in the toaster.

When the false alarm goes off inside of us, it can make us not want to do certain things or not want to go to a certain place. Even though there is no real danger, our body and brain keep telling us there is.

When this happens, it is important that we get back from our 'cave brain' into our 'thinking brain' again. We can do this by:

- Practising the breathing exercises in this book.
- Practising mindfulness.
- Using the calm-down activities in this book or any others we can think of.
- Asking for help and talking about our feelings.

There are other things we can do in our lives all of the time to help us to feel less anxious and worried:

- Get enough sleep.
- Eat regularly and don't eat or drink too much sugar.
- Spend less time on computers, games and electronics.
- Get outdoors and into the fresh air.
- Exercise.
- Laugh and have fun.

Now I know why I feel this way it helps me to know that I am really safe, my brain just gets it wrong sometimes.
A child who struggles with anxiety

# 5. Helping children to express emotions

Children can often find expressing their feelings difficult, particularly with emotions as overwhelming as grief. We can help children learn that expressing emotion can help to relieve these feelings.

There are many ways that we can support a child if they are unable to express themselves verbally. Below are some suggestions. Please feel free to get as creative as you like: change, add, invent, and use what you think might work for the specific child. Children are often the most creative and skilled in being able to 'think outside the box'. Include them in planning what you do – the more they can be included, the more likely they are to engage in it and as a result, feel able to express themselves in a way that is suited to them. If they feel involved, they will get involved.

While using these activities, encourage the child to connect with their experience and how they are feeling: 'I wonder what that sand feels like on your hands? Does it feel warm? Or maybe cool?', or 'I'm wondering how it feels for you when you pound that clay?'.

Try not to interpret what the child may be expressing as we can often get this wrong. Simply accepting what it is that the child is showing you is enough. Allow the child to stay in the metaphor and with the story that they are telling. It is not always important for us to fully understand what the child is expressing, but that we observe and accept it – to help the child to express their emotions freely.

> It is an amazing feeling to see children start to link their feelings and emotions with their body and senses.
> Teaching assistant allocated to provide emotional support to children

## Water and sand

Water can have a soothing quality to it and is really versatile. It can be used alone or with toys and various objects. Glitter, paint or food colouring can be added to it. Often children enjoy simply pouring water from one container to another, and most kitchens have plenty of items that can be used. The water can be used in a washing-up bowl, the sink, the bath tub or a paddling pool – it really doesn't matter – use whatever you have to hand, put down some towels and off they go!

Sand can be equally as soothing as water, and can be used in wet or dry form. Dry sand is great for burying items such as stones, shells, buttons or small toys, for example. As with water, children often enjoy pouring sand from containers or feeling it poured over their hands, which can be relaxing and soothing.

Wet sand allows for children to build more easily: children can make castles, mountains, volcanoes or moats. They may like to use various figures, toys, shells or stones in the sand to tell a story or to play out a scene – they can be as creative as their imagination allows.

# Puppets

Puppets are a really important tool in helping children to express themselves. You can use any kind of puppets – hand, finger, sock, string – it really doesn't matter. The child could even make their own puppets, creating their own characters.

For some children, owning and sharing their thoughts and feelings can be difficult and overwhelming, and often children don't have the words. Puppets can break down some of these barriers and allow children to express themselves through the puppet. The child can share how they are feeling as if it is the puppet's thoughts and feelings. Expressing feelings can be scary, but there is a safety in being vulnerable through the puppet, in exploring emotions through a third person if you like. The child is still able to express themselves but, most importantly, feels safe doing so.

When working with puppets it is important that you play along and stay with what the puppet is telling you, as if it really is the puppet's real thoughts and feelings. For example, if the lion puppet tells you he is angry, you respond to the lion about his feelings of anger, not to the child about their anger. This will hopefully allow the child to continue with their expression and exploration, safe in the knowledge that you believe that they are talking about the feelings and thoughts of the puppet, and not their own.

# Drawing and colouring

Encourage children to draw or colour their feelings. Expressing themselves through art can help children to share, while also keeping an element of privacy.

Scribbling on paper is a great way to express anger or frustration, as well as crumpling it up or tearing it. Throwing away emotions can feel therapeutic for children, as the physical act of 'getting rid of' the unwanted feeling can bring some relief.

# Clay and play dough

Using clay or play dough can be a relaxing, calming way of expressing emotion. The soft, pliable and tactile element of these materials really promotes connection with the senses. You can make your own play dough and add scents and colours to further enhance the experience. Play could be directed, or children could create whatever they like. Children who struggle with perfectionism, or who avoid things for fear or failure, can often feel safe with these materials. There is no right or wrong way to use them, and any perceived mistakes can be easily changed or corrected. Anger can be expressed brilliantly with clay or play dough, which can be pounded, dropped from a height or punched and pinched.

# Music

Movement can help children to express themselves, allowing them to benefit from the health aspect of exercise, as well as encourage the release of endorphins – the human happy hormones. Movement through music can help children to move their bodies and to connect with their body and their feelings. Dancing, listening to music and exercise can all help to alleviate symptoms of anxiety and low mood. You could also incorporate music into drawing, painting, or any of the other activities suggested here.

# Painting

The colours and textures as well as the flowing and mixing of paints can be therapeutic for children and help them to express themselves. You could allow the child to express a particular feeling – to express how they are feeling at the time of painting – or to simply express themselves however they like. Children could use brushes or sponges or, perhaps, their feet or hands to create pictures and help them to get in touch with an earlier stage in their development and simply engage in messy play.

# 6. Memories and special times

## Memories

At times it can be difficult for children to talk about the person who has died. Children may worry that they will forget the person who died or worry that it is too upsetting for others if they talk about that person.

The following activities can help to give the child 'permission' to share their memories, thoughts and feelings of the person who died, as well as help to reassure them that they can use their memories to feel close to the person who died.

*Memory box* – The child could put together a box of memories. They could choose a box that they are drawn to, or maybe decorate a box themselves. Items could include photographs, letters, pictures they have drawn themselves, a CD of songs that remind them of the person, a squirt of (or bottle of) aftershave or perfume, a piece of jewellery, or cufflinks, or anything else that the child would like to add.

*Memory lantern* – For this activity you will need a clear jar, some tissue paper in the child's chosen colours, pens, battery-operated tea lights or fairy lights, and glue. Ask the child to tear or cut up some small pieces of tissue paper. They could write words or memories on them (or draw pictures or memories of the person who died) and talk about each one, if they feel comfortable with this. Ask the child to glue the pieces, one at a time, to the outside of the jar until it is covered. If the child has lots of pieces to add, they can be layered over one another, just as memories are in our minds – they are still there, even if we can't see them. When it is fully covered, put the fairy lights or tea light inside the jar and turn them on.

*Memory tree* – Creating a memory tree can be done in many ways. As a school, having a whole school memory tree can be a great way for children to express all kinds of losses and, over the years, it will slowly fill up. This could be a tree of any description, real or plastic, big or small. It could be a bunch of twigs in a jar full of stones, it really does not matter. Children could hang messages or names on the branches. It could be decorated with keepsakes, fairy lights, wind chimes or anything else that you or the children like.

Alternatively, within the home, a child may want to have their own memory tree to decorate – somewhere for them to hang messages or memories when they like, or one to be used by the whole family, where memories can be shared.

*Memory garden* – Can you help the child to dedicate a section of a garden, yard or outdoor area to the person who died? This could be in the form of a memory flower box, or even a flower pot where a sunflower could be planted in memory of the person, for example. The child can plant seeds and decorate the area with items such as windmills, stones, gems or wind chimes. Create a special place in memory of the person who died, where the child may feel close to them and find some comfort. Remember, though, if it is likely that the child might need to move within the foreseeable future, then they could be distressed by leaving the memory garden behind, in which case one of the portable suggestions would be better.

*Memory stone* – Making memory stones can be done in many ways: the child could collect the stones themselves or, if this is not possible, offer the child a selection of different stones to choose from. The child can choose stones and pebbles they are drawn to, and then decorate them with pens or paints. They can be decorated with words, pictures, colours or messages. Once the child has finished, they could varnish the stones to preserve them. The child could keep the stones or they might like to give them to other members of their family, take them to the person's grave if this is possible, or maybe leave them in a pretty place or somewhere that reminds them of their special person.

*Memory bracelet or Memory key ring* – You could help the child to create their own memory bracelet or key ring. Offer the child a selection of different coloured beads, of various shapes and sizes, and maybe even patterned, if possible. The child could choose any beads they like to represent or remind them of their person or, as a guide, you could suggest examples such as a bead to represent their person's favourite colour, one to represent their personality, a bead that represents a happy memory of their loved person, and one to represent their person's favourite season. Encourage the child to suggest their own reasons for adding beads. These are just ideas, and can help the child to begin the exercise. They may come up with many different, wild and wonderful reasons for adding beads in different colours, shapes and sizes. This can help to make the process all the more personal and special for each individual child. Encourage the child to share their reasons, thoughts and feelings that belong with each bead. In a group setting, children may take it in turns to share their bead creations, helping them to tell their individual story, and also to share with others who may have similar experiences. This can often help to create a sense of belonging and of feeling heard and understood. Alternatively, this may be something that children may wish to create privately, and respecting this is important – they may feel able to share at a later time, or choose to keep this to themselves. It is not hugely important that they should share: the process of creating the memory beads is the most important element.

*Memory jar* – This could be done by the individual child or as a whole family task. The idea is to create a jar full of memories over time. Family members and family friends could also take part. People can add to it at any time, and can also choose a memory from the jar to read themselves or to share with the whole family. It can help families to share memories, and it can also help a lot for them to learn things about their loved one from another person's point of view, things that they might not have known themselves. You simply need a jar, pieces of paper (or card), pens – and memories.

*Salt jar* – Ask the child to choose a coloured chalk to represent a memory or something about their loved one. Show them how to crush the chalk into a fine dust with a rolling pin and to add in the salt until it reaches a colour that they are happy with. Help them to pour it into the jar carefully and ask them to tell you about their memory as they do this. Repeat with various colours representing different memories until the jar is full. Try to keep the jar still and on a flat surface until it is full right to the top (this will help to stop the salt from moving), then the lid can be added and the jar sealed.

I like to keep my Gran's picture by my bed with my memory lantern. Sometimes it makes me cry when I look at them, but I know it's OK to cry now, I don't have to pretend I'm tough all the time.
A 9-year-old girl

# Special times

It is often very important for children that their special person is remembered all year round, but particularly at special times and at various important celebrations throughout the year, such as birthdays, anniversaries, Christmas, Easter, Mother's Day or Father's Day.

Below are some ideas for marking these special occasions:

*Release balloons or lanterns* – Releasing balloons or lanterns can be a powerful experience for children: it can be a way of sending a message to their loved one, releasing emotion or saying goodbye, to name a few. Children might wish to attach a letter or a picture they have drawn to the balloon or to draw on the balloon itself.

*Drawing pictures* – Making cards or writing poems or letters can be important for children to mark these occasions. Adults can help by laminating them, if possible, so that children can feel secure leaving them at the person's grave, where their ashes are scattered or any other outdoor places, knowing that they will be protected from the elements. They could also be added to the child's memory box.

*Planting* – Children could plant seeds in memory of their person, which they can tend to and watch grow. This could be part of a memory garden, or simply in a plant pot.

*Christmas decoration* – Children could decorate a Christmas bauble or choose a beautiful decoration to hang on the Christmas tree in memory of their special person.

*Light a candle* – With full adult supervision – a candle could be lit in memory of the person who died. This is not just a religious concept; I have known many children who have found comfort in doing this in memory of their special person.

Most importantly, try talking to the child about the person who died, especially at these times. Even if the child doesn't mention them, the chances are that they are thinking about them. Also keep in mind events such as school assemblies, the first days at a new school or in a new year group, and parents' evenings – these aren't necessarily classed as 'special occasions' to you or me, but to a child these can often be very special, and they can be times when the child might miss the person who died the most.

> I know it's OK for us all to talk about their Mum together. We don't have to worry about upsetting each other, because it's OK to be upset and show it and to all remember their Mum as a family.
> Parent whose partner passed away

# 7. Breathing

*You will need*: a soft toy, art materials, pipe cleaners, paper cup, toilet roll and balloons.

We can use breathing practice to help children to learn to self-soothe when they are experiencing overwhelming emotion.

Deep breathing can:

- Help us to calm our body and mind.
- Reduce the stress hormone cortisol.
- Help to slow our breathing rate.
- Decrease our heart rate.

There are many different ways to help children to practise deep breathing, and I have always found that it is certainly not a case of 'one size fits all'. Children are drawn to different techniques and finding what works for them is very important in encouraging them use these skills. Children can add these exercises to their own 'first aid kit' to be used whenever they need to.

We can teach children to identify how they are feeling by teaching them to tune in to their body and breath. You can practise different types of breathing with the child and explore how they feel afterwards. You can talk about what your 'normal' breathing looks like when you aren't thinking about it. Or discuss how slow and steady breathing feels compared to fast, shallow breathing.

As with any new skill, practice makes perfect. The more a child can practise these techniques when they are feeling calm, the more comfortable they will feel using them. The hope is that the child will then use the techniques when they start to feel overwhelmed.

## 5, 4, 3, 2, 1

Ask the child to name:

5 things I can see
4 things I can feel
3 things I can hear
2 things I can smell
1 thing I can taste

# Super pose

This is a great way of helping children to ground or calm themselves, as well as a way to boost self-confidence and help them to feel more empowered. Ask the child to stand how a super hero might stand. Ask the child to show you *and* to describe the position, and then do a checklist inventory:

> Legs hip-width apart, check; feet flat on the floor, check; hands on hips, check; or one hand on hip and one extended in the air, proudly, check; back straight, check; chest out, check; chin up, check.

If the child is not naturally standing how you have described they will more than likely adjust their position as you go through the checklist. You could ask the child how they feel before they adopt the position, and then again after they have held it for 30 seconds.

# Pinwheels

Children often enjoy having visual and physical aids to help them to learn. They can help the child to begin to notice their breathing and take more of an interest in doing so. Pinwheels can be used to help with this. Ask the child to use their breath to make it spin slowly and quickly or to keep it spinning for the longest time they can.

# Belly breathing

Ask the child to sit or lie somewhere comfortable and place their hand on their chest or stomach. Direct them to notice the rise and fall as they take some slow, deep breaths. Ask the child to imagine that they have a balloon inside their belly. Ask them to imagine that when they breathe in the balloon fills with air, ask them to breathe in deeply so that the balloon fills up and makes their belly fill up. Now ask them to slowly let out all of the air in the balloon and to notice how their belly goes back down again. You could also ask children to lie on the ground and place a soft toy on their stomach. The child will be able to watch it rise and fall as they breathe in and out slowly, remind them to make sure that they keep breathing steadily – to keep the soft toy balanced.

# Stan breathing

We are going to use Stan the Giraffe to do some calm Stan breathing.

Begin by standing with your feet slightly apart, take a few deep breaths in and out, in and out, that's it. Now we are going to imagine we have a very long neck just like Stan. When we breathe in, we are going to imagine the air going all the way down our long giraffe neck and into our lungs. Try that now, imagining the air travelling all the way down your long neck. Do this twice more, nice and slowly, that's it.

Now, the next time you breathe in I want you to stretch your arms up high in the sky, nice and slowly. Keep them there just for a few breaths, and when you are ready, on your next out breath, slowly bend forwards and bring your arms down towards your toes. Relax there for a few breaths like a giraffe munching on some grass.

When you are ready slowly start to stand back up straight again. If you feel sad or scared or angry, you can use your Stan breathing to help you to relax and feel calmer.

# Balloon breathing

CAUTION! If you choose this activity please ensure it is done under full adult supervision, and children are not left alone with balloons at any point – they are a choking hazard.

Ask the child to tell you their worries. For each worry, you or the child can blow a breath into the balloon. If you're confident with how the child is feeling, they can blow the breath themselves, otherwise you can do it for them. Breathe the worries into the balloons using slow and steady breaths. Completing this activity with a child can help to link it to the slow and steady breathing required when they become anxious. You can gently remind them to do their 'balloon breathing'.

Once the balloon is full it can then be:

- Released to zoom around the room – demonstrating the worries shrinking in size as they fall out of the balloon.
- Tied and then popped with a pin to help the child to gain power and control over their worries.

Alternatively, you or the child could write feelings on pieces of paper and put them inside the balloon. Once the balloon has been blown up, it can then be popped: again, giving the child a metaphorical power over the feelings they are experiencing and empowering them to take some control back.

Another option is for you or the child to write feelings on the outside of the balloon with a marker pen. Then repeat the actions above, either releasing it to deflate it or popping it.

> I can feel calm again, I just have to breathe.
> 7-year-old girl

# 8. Relaxation

*You will need*: a comfortable place to sit or lie; blankets and cushions are optional.

The following exercises can help children learn how to relax their bodies and minds. Please note, some children may not wish to close their eyes as part of these activities and it is important for us to respect their choice. They can still take part and you may ask if they are comfortable to sit facing away from you, or any other possible distractions, so that they are able to focus. Children may feel too vulnerable to close their eyes but it may be something that they are able to build up to over time.

## Under the sea

This exercise is a guided meditation to help children to relax and find a calm place within their own heads. It can also demonstrate the power of imagination, and help children to learn the skills of relaxation as well as of using their inner resources. There is a script below that you can either follow or adapt to make longer or shorter. There are also lots of examples of other guided meditations online or you could write your own, tailored to the child's interests. Please read it in a calm, relaxed voice, ensuring you have plenty of time. Read through it slowly, pausing often to allow the child to visualise the scene and really experience and take it in. Guided meditation can be particularly helpful at bedtime to help a child to switch their mind off and settle to sleep.

> We are going to use our imagination now. Our imagination can be very powerful, and we are going to practise using it to help us to relax and feel good. The more we practise using our imagination in this way, the easier it becomes – a bit like riding a bike. The more we practise it the better we become at it, and the easier it becomes. The same happens with our imagination: the more we use it, the bigger and stronger it becomes and the easier it is to use.

> First of all, get into a comfortable position, this might be lying down or sitting comfortably. Now, I am going to ask you to close your eyes and take a deep breath in ... and release. Breathe in ... and release. Keep concentrating on breathing in and out, slowly and deeply.

> We are going to go deep under the sea. Because we are using our imagination, we don't have to hold our breath, we can breathe under the sea, like mermaids or mermen, and we are all great swimmers, in our imagination.

> Imagine you are sitting on the edge of a rock, with your legs dangling in the clear, blue, warm water below. ... You can smell the salty water and the seaweed on the rocks. ... When you are ready, push yourself off the rock into the warm, salty sea ... did you hear the splash the water made ...?

Imagine yourself swimming down to the seabed below, what can you see ...? Can you see the fish swimming around you ...? Feel them swimming past your arms and legs, they have come to say hello. ... Can you reach out and touch them gently ...? Can you see the bright colours of the fish ...? The blues, the reds, the greens, the yellows and the orange colours ...? Fish of all shapes, sizes and colours, the most unusual fish you can imagine. ...

Oh, there's a rainbow fish ... and over there you can see an octopus. ... What colour is it ...? Can you see the tentacles moving with the current ...? Listen to the underwater sounds ... swoosh ... swoosh ...

Oh, look over there, there's the coral reef ... look at the beautiful colours of the coral: pink, orange, red. ... The fish are swimming all around the coral. Can you see them ...? In and out of the cracks and gaps. Playing hide and seek ...

Look at the sea bed ... you can see lots of beautiful shells ... bend down and pick some up ... feel how smooth one of them is ... and how rough the other one is in your hand ...

It's time to go back to the surface now ... you gently start to swim back up to the surface of the water ... kicking your arms and legs gently as you move slowly back up towards the world above. ... As your head reaches the top of the water you take a big deep breath ... and gently open your eyes again. ... You can remember your time under the sea, and know that you only need to close your eyes and you can return to your secret, underwater world whenever you wish to.

As an extension exercise, children could draw, paint or describe what they visualised in their underwater world. This can help children to recall and enhance what they were able to imagine, and also act as a visual reminder of a time that they felt calm and relaxed.

# Still like a tree

This guided relaxation script can help children to find calm within chaos. It can help children to feel more grounded, even when they are feeling wobbly. Practising this regularly with children may mean that they are able to use the imagery whenever they need to feel grounded, even without someone reading the script.

Read the script slowly, in a calm, soothing voice, pausing regularly to allow the child chance to really engage with the descriptions.

Stand up and take a deep breath in, as you breathe in, feel it filling up your lungs and as you let it go, feel your shoulders relax gently. Do this again ... and again.

Keep breathing deeply and calmly and when you take another breath, imagine you are a tall, strong, sturdy tree. Imagine that your spine is the tree trunk running down to your legs and then on down to your feet. Feel your feet on the ground, keeping you safe and connected to the earth. Imagine you have roots coming from the bottom of your feet like a tree. When you next breathe out, imagine the roots burying deep into the ground and spreading out like fingers. You can feel the wind gently blowing your branches high in the sky, but the roots below are keeping you safe and strong. Imagine as you breathe in that you bring calm energy up from the ground up through your roots, into your feet, up your legs and up through the rest of your body and branches.

When you are feeling relaxed and calm, slowly open your eyes. Gently lift one foot just off the ground, put it back down and then lift the other, take a few tiny, slow steps moving from side to side where you are standing.

Practise this tree exercise so that when you feel that you need to calm yourself, you can do this no matter where you are.

Bedtimes can be the most difficult time of day for all of us. Reading a guided meditation to my son when he gets into bed helps him to fall asleep quicker. It helps me relax too.
Parent of a 5-year-old whose sister passed away

# 9. Mindfulness

Mindfulness is the act of being present and in the moment. It is taking a few minutes to focus on what is happening for you, within you and around you. It can calm your body and mind and bring peace.

The more that mindfulness is practised and incorporated into everyday life, the easier it is to access and the more natural it will become. A child will very often live in the moment, however, sometimes that child can become 'stuck' in their head. This can be more likely if they have experienced something that has caused feelings of anxiety, such as trauma or loss. When this happens, the child can sometimes become disconnected from their body. Mindfulness can help them to reconnect gently.

Mindfulness can help children to accept their feelings, to learn that they don't have to ignore them, or feel scared or ashamed of them, or even change how they feel. Mindfulness can also help children to notice that all feelings come and go.

Mindfulness can promote self-esteem and resilience, as well as reduce anxiety, stress and aggression. Concentration, emotional control and empathy can also be improved. It is beneficial for adults (think self-care), as well as for children. Practising mindfulness yourself is the best way to encourage children to engage too.

There are many different ways to promote and incorporate mindfulness into everyday life, below are some ideas.

## Mindful eating

*You will need*: a few small pieces of the food of your choice – ensure the child is not allergic to the chosen food, and try to choose something that you think the child will want to eat.

Talk to the child about the last thing they had to eat, it might have been their breakfast, or maybe they have had their lunch or a snack. Ask them if they noticed anything about the food they ate, if they could describe the taste to you, the texture, the smell, what it looked like, did it make any sound when they chewed it? The chances are the child may not be able to be very descriptive at all.

Explain that you would like them to do some mindful eating with you.

First ask them to look at the piece of food, what colours can they see, are there many different colours? Does it look smooth or bumpy, shiny or dull? Does it look tasty? Is there anything else you can see when you look at it?

Next ask the child to pick it up; you can also do the same with your piece of food. Ask them what it feels like? Does it feel how they thought it would? Is it rough, smooth, soft, squishy, hard or bumpy? Ask them to touch it, move it around in their hands and run their fingers over it.

Ask the child to put it by their ear. Can you hear anything if you rub or squeeze it or if you tap it with your finger?

Encourage the child to smell it. Can you take a deep sniff in through your nose? Does the smell remind you of anything? Do you like the smell? Is it a strong smell or a gentle smell?

Explain to the child that they aren't going to eat it straight away, but ask them to put it on their lips, what does it feel like? Ask them to take a small bite and move it around inside their mouth. Can they taste any flavours? Can they taste it on their tongue? Ask the child to take another bite and do the same again. Then they may take a bigger bite and continue eating the whole thing, slowly and calmly, noticing the flavours as they do.

Once the child has finished, you could talk about the difference between that experience and the one they told you about before you started. Ask if they enjoyed the food more because they were noticing the sight, smell, sound, taste and texture, or if it was frustrating and they wanted to gobble it down. Try to bring the child's attention to the whole experience, and any feelings and emotions they noticed.

# Body scan

*You will need*: a comfortable place to sit or lie, blankets and cushions are optional.

Lie down or sit comfortably. We are going to do a body scan, by pretending you are in a body scanning machine. Close your eyes if you feel comfortable to, and take in some slow, deep breaths, just like we practised. Breathe in … and out … and in … and out. Now, imagine the machine is just above your toes: how do your toes and feet feel? Are they comfortable in your shoes and socks? Do they feel warm or cool? Don't try to change anything about how they feel, just notice.

The machine is moving up over your legs now, notice how they feel, are they comfortable where you are sitting/lying? Can you feel your clothes against your legs? Can you feel the ground/chair against your legs? Again, we aren't changing anything, we are just noticing how our legs feel, and getting in touch with our body.

The machine is slowly moving up to your tummy, back and chest now. I wonder if you can feel your heart beating? Can you feel your tummy moving up and down as you breathe in and out? I wonder how your back is feeling against the chair/ground. Are there any other feelings you can notice? Don't try to change anything, just notice and observe what is going on.

The machine moves up for the final time up over your neck, face and head. What can you notice now? Are the muscles in your face relaxed or tense? Can you feel your scalp, the top of your head? What about your throat as you breathe and swallow? Just take a few seconds here to notice anything at all.

We are going to stay here for a few more seconds, breathing slowly and gently. Now, when you are ready, I want you to wiggle your fingers and toes and slowly open your eyes.

# Bell

*You will need*: a bell: a singing bowl, or a meditation bell would work well; and apps are also available, which play similar relaxing sounds.

Ask the child to sit quietly and comfortably, explain that you are going to ring a bell and would like them to listen carefully to the ringing sound. Ask them to stay quiet all the way through, and just to put their hand in the air when they can't hear the bell ringing any longer. Tell the child that when they have done this, you would like them to stay silent for just a little bit longer, so they can notice any other sounds that they can hear.

Ring the bell and observe the child's response. Does this appear difficult for the child, are they able to engage? Once the bell has finished ringing, give the child some further time to observe sounds around them.

Ask the child to tell you about any sounds they could hear and what the experience was like for them.

# Mindful colouring

*You will need*: colouring sheets/books, pens, pencils or crayons.

Mindful colouring can help to provide relief from stress and anxiety as it can promote a relaxed, almost meditative, state. It can help people to focus on the present moment as they focus on the task at hand and can bring release from negative thoughts and emotions.

There are many, many books full of intricate pictures and beautiful mandalas that you can purchase or download from the internet. There is also a picture of Stan the Giraffe on the following page that can be photocopied and used to help introduce children to mindful colouring.

> I like it when I notice my feelings by doing mindfulness, it helps me to remember that I will feel calm again soon.
> 8-year-old boy whose Mum passed away

# Mindful colouring: Stan the Giraffe

*You will need*: colouring pencils and Stan outline.

# 10. Other activities

## Colour your feelings

Stan the Giraffe feels lots of different emotions throughout the story and his colours change showing how he is feeling.

Can you colour your feelings?

# Emotion words

| | | |
|---|---|---|
| Happy | Cheerful | Satisfied |
| Lonely | Alone | Terrific |
| Calm | Delighted | Relaxed |
| Confused | Silly | Unloved |
| Afraid | Thankful | Mean |
| Responsible | Sad | Gloomy |
| Worried | Grateful | Blue |
| Uncomfortable | Bored | Frustrated |
| Destructive | Glad | Disappointed |
| Furious | Excited | Hurt |
| Awful | Loved | Embarrassed |
| Confident | Proud | Scared |
| Content | Courageous | Miserable |
| Angry | Ashamed | Kind |
| Irritated | Quiet | Jealous |
| Insecure | Curious | Guilty |
| Shy | Generous | Worried |
| Surprised | Ignored | Peaceful |
| Brave | Impatient | Stubborn |
| Friendly | Interested | Relieved |
| Overwhelmed | Loving | Energetic |

Using emotion cards can help children to develop their emotional language and understanding. It can also help adults to identify areas where the child may struggle.

There are so many different ways to use emotion cards with children. They can easily be used with an individual child or in bigger groups. Below are some suggestions, but please feel free to invent your own ways of using them too.

You can make your own cards or photocopy the words on the previous page onto coloured card for example, cut them out and even laminate them if you want them to last a long time. This is not an exhaustive list, there are many, many more that can be added, and the children may have suggestions too.

- Choose a card and say what a person might think if they were feeling like this.
- Choose a card and act out a scene where someone might be feeling like this.
- Choose a card and describe it to another person, without saying what the feeling is, and see if they can guess it.
- Choose a card and talk about how their body might feel if they were feeling this emotion.
- Choose a card and talk about what the person might do if they wanted to change the way they were feeling.
- Choose a card and talk about the meaning.

# In and out

*You will need*: colouring materials, face shapes or paper plates

As humans, we often show the world one version of ourselves and keep the real us hidden from view. We also do this with emotions, so this exercise is to help children to express what is inside of them, and what is outside.

Children can use the picture on the next page to draw, colour or write words or symbols: they can use one side of the head to represent what they allow others to see, and the other side, to represent what they hide. You could direct them to focus on emotions, or how they see themselves and how others see them.

It could also be useful to use masks to help to explore this. Children could design and make their own masks, or you could have some pre-prepared, perhaps downloaded from the internet or some oval shapes you have drawn. Paper plates could also be used for this activity.

Using masks can help to demonstrate the actual physical act of hiding our inner selves, thoughts, feelings and emotions with an outer 'mask'. Talking about how clowns paint on a 'mask' that can show they are happy (or sad) can also demonstrate this: How might the clown feel underneath the mask? Do they always feel as happy (or sad) as their face paint suggests?

# Jigsaw of me

*You will need*: a large sheet of paper, outline of the body, scissors and colouring materials. Emotion cards are optional.

This activity is to encourage children to reflect on their physical feelings, as well as their emotions, as they experience them within their body. There is an outline on the following page that can be divided into sections and used as a jigsaw. Consider the child's ability before choosing how many sections to divide the body into.

Give the child a pre-cut jigsaw in the shape of a human body. Ask the child to write an emotion or physical feeling on each piece of the jigsaw as they piece it back together. If they find emotions difficult to express, or have a limited vocabulary, you could use emotion cards as a prompt. This can be a great opportunity to help expand the child's emotional vocabulary and understanding by talking through the meanings of each word as it is used. Offering examples of times when people may experience such emotions can be helpful, and might also encourage the child to share their experiences of different emotions too.

Alternatively, you could ask the child to lie on a large sheet of paper if they wish to, while you draw around their outline. They could then divide the shape into separate jigsaw pieces and complete the activity as above.

If they struggle with this activity, you could suggest that the child uses colours or shapes to represent their emotions. Once they begin to express them in this way, they may then be able to share them more verbally, but if not, simply respect this and allow them to continue. It is not always important for us to know what the child is feeling, particularly if the child is not yet aware What is important is that they are able to express themselves safely and without judgement.

You can link in physical feelings to this too by focusing on one emotion at a time. For example, exploring how they physically feel grief within their body, and where they feel it – some children may find that their legs ache, for others, their head might hurt. There are many physical feelings throughout the body that can be shared and explored.

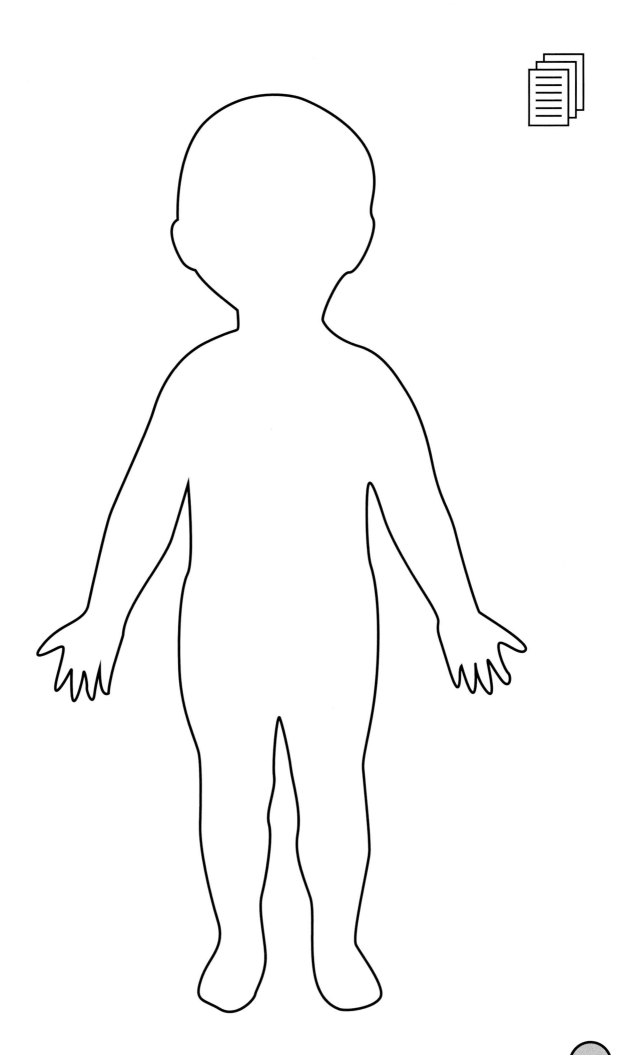

# The moon

In the story, Stan the Giraffe finds hope and love again when he sees the moon. He knows he will never forget the sun that is so special to him, but the moon helps Stan to feel peaceful and hopeful again.

Who or what brings you hope and love? Or helps you to feel peaceful?

Draw, write or colour in the moon.

# Pillowcase comfort

*You will need*: card, a plain pillowcase and fabric pens.

Often when a loved one has died, children can experience unsettled sleep. Lying in bed can be a time when they are not distracted and thoughts and feelings can often surface. They may have been used to their loved one putting them to bed or the family routine may have changed due to the death. It may also be one of the only times during the day that the child is on their own, and does not have the comfort of being around others. There are many, many things that can make bedtime and sleep difficult.

Some children might find comfort in having a photograph of their loved one by their bed or under their pillow. Some find that having something that belonged to their loved one can bring them some comfort, perhaps a teddy or an item of clothing.

Some children have found that designing and creating a pillowcase using fabric pens can be beneficial. Children can write messages, words, add colours or draw pictures. The child can be as creative as they like. The pillowcase can also be taken on school trips, holidays or sleepovers; times when there is more change for the child.

A set of fabric pens and a plain pillowcase is all that is needed for this activity. Insert a piece of card inside the pillowcase so that the design doesn't bleed through onto the other side. Children may like to decorate both sides.

# The rock

At one point in the story, Stan the Giraffe is really angry. He is so angry that he kicks a rock high into the sky.

What makes you feel like kicking things or makes you feel super-angry?

You could draw what makes you angry or any feelings that you would like to throw away.

Draw them onto the rock on the next page.

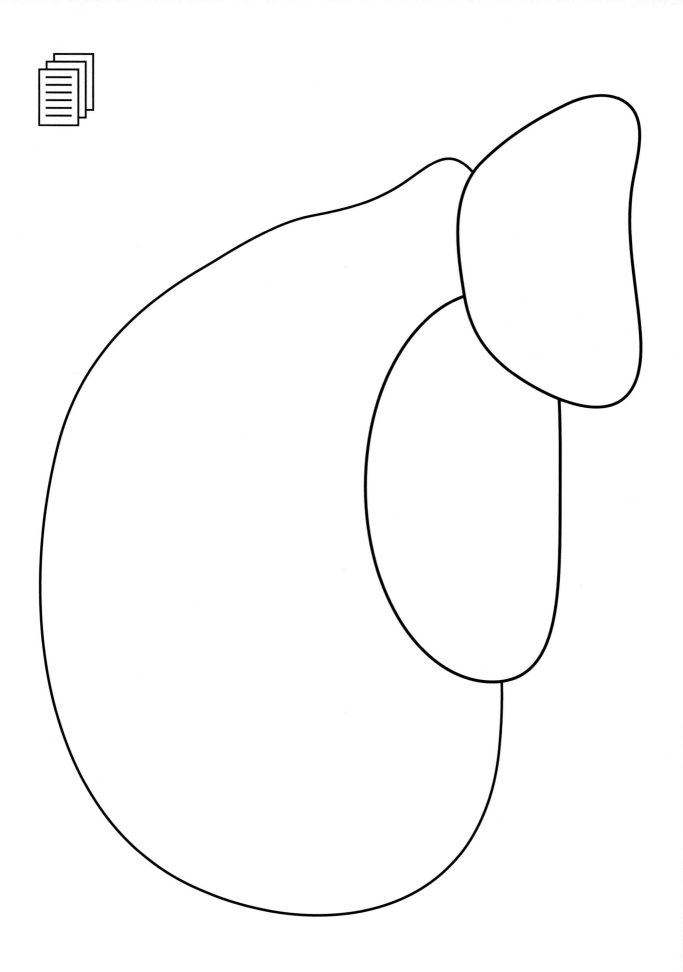

# 11. Group work

It is important to recognise that any group work that is undertaken is not classed as group therapy. Group therapy should only be undertaken by a qualified therapist. The groups I will talk about are simply for children who will, hopefully, feel a sense of understanding from others who may have a shared experience and who can provide an opportunity for children to learn.

Often, having the opportunity to share thoughts, feelings and emotions in a safe environment, as well as sharing stories, can be cathartic, particularly when meeting with those who have had similar experiences.

When supporting children with bereavement in a group situation, it is important to consider many things. I have addressed below some of those I feel are important and need to be considered prior to any group work being undertaken. These are things that I have found have worked for me and the children I have supported when delivering group work. However, this is your group, so please change things to make it work for your children.

## Preparation

There are many practicalities that need to be clear, such as who will facilitate and co-facilitate the group, and how many children will attend. My experience is that at least two facilitators need to be present and roughly six to eight children. It is important to select the right facilitators to run the group and ensure that they work well together, complementing one another. Recognise the strengths and limitations of each person and ensure that their personalities and skills lend themselves well to the task at hand. People need to have a certain level of resilience, as well as being able to demonstrate empathy, acceptance and understanding.

Consider how often the group will run, when it will be held, and for how long. My groups have always been run each week on the same day and at the same time, for an hour, over 8 weeks. Consistency of day and time can be hugely important for children to feel safe and secure. If you are working in a school, you may need to discuss times with staff to ensure children are able to miss certain lessons without a huge impact on their schooling.

Consider where it will be held. My advice would be in a room where there are limited distractions, where the group will not be interrupted and, ideally, the same room each week. I understand it is often very difficult to find appropriate spaces, but somewhere that is big enough for the children to move around when needed, yet without being vast, is great. Somewhere children can feel safe. It would be helpful to have space for children to sit on the floor, but also to have the option of chairs and tables, which could be pushed up against the walls and then used as and when needed.

The make-up of the group needs to be considered carefully. Is this a group to reflect on 'losses'? You may have children who have had a parent move away or a family member imprisoned, or who are struggling with a sibling's move to university, as well as children who are bereaved. Or is this a group made up solely of children who are bereaved?

Before the group begins, it is important that discussions with children and their parents, carers and teachers are held to prepare each child for the group. This will help the children to understand the purpose of the group and what it will entail. It is important for them to know how long the group will run for, roughly how many people will take part, who will run it for them and when and where it will be held. It may be appropriate to discuss what it is you hope the child may get out of coming to the group, as well as there being an opportunity for them to say what they would like to get from taking part and, most importantly, if they actually want to take part.

It is also important that group members do not change: children may choose to leave the group, but it is important for group dynamics that new members are not introduced; this can unsettle children and leave them feeling unsafe.

It is important for facilitators to factor in time to debrief at the end of each session. This allows them time to reflect on how the session went, if they would want to change anything, and to process their learning from the session. It is also an opportunity to reflect on their own feelings and experience, which is imperative to ensure that they are able to facilitate the group effectively.

# Running the group

Make sure you are prepared for each session, with a plan of your session, any feedback to be given, and any props or creative materials that you may need. Activity times can vary depending on many factors, such as age of the group members, the number of children in the group, and the children's ability to focus, to name just a few. Tailor the timing of each activity specifically to your individual group. You may also wish to have a few 'back up' ideas to hand, in case you need to shift the mood, either to calm the group down or to re-energise the group. You will need to include an element of flexibility. Although you will have prepared an outline, it is impossible to know what will come up during the session or what may need to be changed. Being open to change, having an ability to think on your feet, and, most importantly, to respond to the needs of the children in the group, is a huge part of being able to facilitate a group successfully.

At the beginning of a group it is essential to set group boundaries and rules. Children are extremely good at understanding why we need rules, and also in suggesting rules for the group. It can be useful to write these on a large sheet of paper that can be kept for the duration of the group and put on the wall each week, so it can be referred back to when it is needed.

It can also be helpful to create a group identity, in which case the children can give themselves a group name, group symbol or create a group poster, if they wish to do so, and if you feel this is appropriate. This can be a bonding experience for the group, but do try to ensure that the ideas and suggestions of all members are considered.

Creating routine and rituals that are repeated regularly during the group can help the group to unite, and help children to feel safe within it.

Opening and closing rounds: as well as becoming a ritual, these can help children to begin the group, to share and open up, as well as to close and mark the ending once the session is over. The ending or closing round can act as a signal for the group, allowing children to share anything they wish to before the session ends. It is important to try to make the transition to the next part of the day calm and peaceful for the children.

Using statements in the group can help children to share and explore feelings, for example 'I feel sad when ...'. However, the statements can often become distorted or turned into something completely different, as each child takes a turn to answer and, once changed, the next child may then follow this new statement. Sometimes these changes of statements can be helpful, as it is something that is important to the child, but at other times, the changes can move away from the intention of the round. Having the statements written down or printed on pieces of card or paper and visible in the middle of the group can be helpful. The statement can then be referred back to by those running the group, or by the children themselves, as a prompt.

The use of talking while holding an object can often be helpful in a group situation. This indicates visually to the children whose turn it is to talk and share, and can be used as a prompt when children are not taking turns or when talking over one another.

Using a puppet as the talking object can also serve another purpose: if something is difficult to share, children can choose for the puppet to talk on their behalf. Puppets can help children to communicate through metaphor and allow them to speak without taking full ownership of what is being shared.

Children are given the option to choose not to share if they do not wish to. Although we would encourage and hope that children would wish to join in, it is their free choice not to do so. Providing that they are not disrupting others or causing issues, children can still benefit from listening to others and being in the group environment. If a child chooses not to share, you can give them another opportunity once the other children have taken their turn. It might be that given a second opportunity, they feel better able to share. This should be outlined in the group expectations at the beginning of the group, so that children know they can choose to opt out and will be offered another chance after the others. It is important that the rest of the group are aware that this is the individual's choice and that they need to respect this decision.

Giving children feedback from the previous session at the beginning of each new session can be very powerful. It can help children to start on a positive note, and can help to reinforce positive characteristics or behaviours that you would like to encourage within the group. It can also help children to feel reassured that you have held them in mind between sessions. Feedback needs to be specific and realistic.

There is also the opportunity to give group feedback too: this can support the group's development and help members of the group to recognise movement and bonding within the group, as well as help to identify the positives that can be obtained from group work. Statements such as this – 'As a group, you were very honest with each other and you listened really well to each other' – may be appropriate. If there has been a difficult group session, positives can still be found without being dishonest, for example: 'Taking turns was sometimes difficult last week, but the group members were very keen to share their feelings'; or 'You helped each other last week by …'.

# Structure

It can be helpful to follow the same basic structure for each session; this can help to bring a familiarity to the group and a sense of rhythm. Again, this is your group, you can change and adapt these suggestions to meet the needs of your group.

*Check in* – Find out how children are right now. This could be an energy level (1 being no energy and 10 being bursting with energy), a word, a sentence or a colour to describe their mood, a weather forecast, or a type of animal that represents how they are feeling – it could be anything you like. Choose what works for your group of children. You could also include feedback at this point.

*Ice breaker* – This could be a variety of different activities, there are some examples on the following pages. They can be used to welcome children to the session each week and to set the scene for the main activity. Often, using statements at this point can be useful, for example: 'I feel scared/lonely/angry/sad/happy/lonely/safe when …', 'I wish …', 'One thing that really annoys me is …', 'I am noisy when …' or 'If I was a colour/animal/shape/car I would be …'.

*Main activity* – This is the main body of the work and is where the children may take part in something geared more towards the aim of the group, exploring and sharing their stories or emotions. These activities need to be well thought out and planned and children need to feel safe in order to take part. Towards the end of the 8 weeks, the members may feel more comfortable sharing within the group.

*Relief activity* – This could be fun or calming, depending on the need. What you choose at this point depends entirely on the mood of the group and whether the mood needs to be changed slightly. If the mood is heavy and low, it might be that an activity or game that requires physical movement is required, or if the group members are over-excited then a more calming activity might be chosen. Be prepared to be flexible. My advice would be to have plenty to choose from to enable you to respond to the needs of the group.

*Check out* – My experience has been positive when using the same method of check in and check out. This can often help to gauge for us, and the children, how each child's mood, as well as the group's mood, may have changed during the session. You could also ask children to reflect on something they have learned or will take away and use from the session. Some children like to incorporate a 'feelings bin'. A small bin or basket that can be used to throw away any emotions that they want to leave behind. Children don't have to share these with anyone else, and these emotions can be written on paper and then crumpled or torn up or simply put in the 'feelings bin'.

# Ice breakers and relief activities

As well as being used for group bonding and breaking the ice, these activities can also be used as light relief. They can be used to change the mood, to teach children skills or to just be enjoyable for children to take part in. Below are some examples and there are also activities in the main body of the book that can be used. (See Chapters 5 to 10.)

*People bingo* – This can help children to start building relationships and possibly to find some common ground. Children could have a tick list or a bingo sheet and, for example, find a person who: can whistle, likes dogs, or likes dancing. Ask them to move around the room and ask the other group members. If they find someone who ticks off something from their list then they can move to another person, and continue to move around the group until their list is complete. You can set an allotted time for the task and stop the task if the children begin to struggle to complete the list.

*Mix up* – The group sit in a circle while you name each of them with a variety of different sweet names: for example: lollipop, bubblegum and chocolate buttons. When you say the name of a sweet those children swap places. When you say 'mix up' they all have to move seats.

*Guess the mime* – Take turns to mime an action: for example, digging, singing, dancing or eating. Whoever guesses correctly then takes a turn.

*Pass the ...* – Children sit in a circle, you instruct them to pass a slap (hands slapped on floor), click, clap or stamp around the circle, in the order of how they are sitting. If someone misses their turn or does the action when it is not their turn, the whole group starts again. See if they can get good at this, working together to get faster, change direction and so on.

*Copy action* – Identify one child to start off. They choose an action, for example clapping, and the whole group copy. Identify another child to choose something else, for example stamping, and so it continues. You could add in rhythms and patterns or strike a pose and take turns to choose the pose.

*Remote control* – You can use an actual remote for this is you like, but an imaginary one is also fine. Tell the children that you have a remote control with different buttons on it that direct how to move. The buttons on the remote control are: Play – walking straight ahead at a normal pace; Stop – signals the end of the game; Pause – stop for a moment; Slow motion – walk forwards very slowly; and Rewind – walk backwards slowly. Once the children become used to these instructions you could then add in some other buttons such as jumping, skipping, and such like.

*Guess what* – Children take it in turns to act out the use of an everyday object or activity using a pen (or another object of your choice) to help them, for example: brushing your teeth (the pen could be the toothbrush) or using an umbrella (the pen could be the handle of the umbrella). The children act this out in silence and the other children guess. Once it has been guessed, the next child takes their turn and so on.

# Main activities

These are some suggestions for the main body of the group session. There are also many activities suggested in the main part of this book that can be adapted to be used in a group setting. The mindfulness and breathing activities can be used and repeated weekly. This allows the children to practise them within the group, which should encourage them to use them when needed. The relaxation exercises also work well in a group setting (see Chapter 8).

# Parachute game: riding the waves

*You will need*: a parachute and some balls.

The group members sit around the outside of the parachute. Before you begin, talk to the children about grief coming in waves. Some days the waves feel big and strong and there are lots of them washing over you. On days like this you might feel lots of emotions washing over you too. On other days the waves are smaller and more gentle. Some days you might have big waves and little waves all at different times, and this is OK too. Sometimes these waves of grief might come over you all of a sudden when you weren't expecting them. Emotions of grief can come and go, just like the waves on the sea, and just like the ball, we have to learn to ride the waves when they come.

Ask the children to stand up, spread out and hold a piece of the parachute with each hand. Put a ball on the parachute, the aim is for the children to keep the ball on the parachute. Tell the children what the waves are like, and ask the children make the waves using the parachute. You might start off with some small, gentle waves and build up to stormy seas, before calming again to a gentle ripple. Children could take it in turns to give the instruction to the rest of the group, and you could add more balls to make it more difficult to keep them on the parachute.

# Group art

*You will need*: large sheets of paper, paints, paint brushes, pallets, water. Other art materials are optional.

Lay out a large roll or big sheets of paper joined together end to end, and instruct the group to create something together using paints. You could give them a theme: for example, beginnings, endings, their experience during the group, seasons or loss.. Or you could ask the group to decide together what they would like to create. Give the group a set time limit and tell them that you will let them know when they have ten minutes left, and again when they have five minutes left. Ask that all members take part in the activity and that all are to have a say in what they decide to create.

You may also wish to do this early on in the group process, and then repeat again in the end session. This is a really good way of demonstrating how far the group has come, and how much more able they are now to work together as a team than they might have been able to at the beginning.

You could also provide other art materials: pens, pencils, pastels, feathers and buttons or whatever you like. Just ensure you have enough time to allow them to complete this.

# Maze

*You will need*: pens and maze photocopies.

Children can often relate to metaphors that we use to describe grief. Some children will understand the description of grief being like the sea, sometimes it is calm and other days it is stormy, and sometimes it is a mixture of both.

Describing grief to be like a maze can also be useful. Using the maze on the next page as you talk about grief can help children to grasp the concept. Give each child a photocopied maze picture and pencil, so that they can try to find their way to the end. Explain to them how grief can be like a maze: you can't see the end, there are lots of times when we might feel like we are going in the wrong direction, we can take wrong turns, and come up against walls or other difficulties, and yet at other times we move forwards. Sometimes we need to ask for help to find our way through the maze, and that is OK.

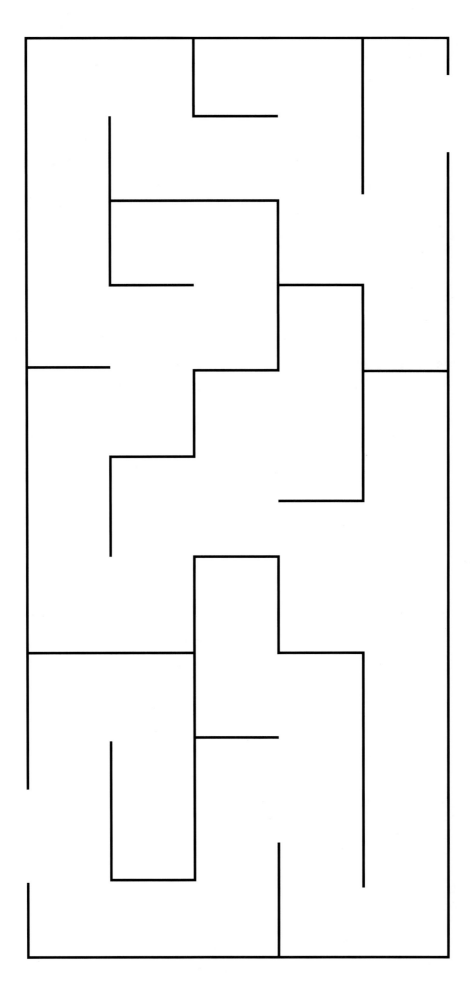

# Make a memory sculpture

*You will need*: modelling clay or play dough.

Give the children the task of creating something that reminds them of the person who died: it might be a memory they have of them, or maybe something they used to do with the person, anything at all they like. Before they begin, ask the children to consider if they would like to share their creation and memory with the group at the end, but that reassure them that it is OK not to, if they prefer. Once the children have finished, invite them to share with the group. They can take their creations home with them.

# Mirror mirror

Pair the children up with a partner. Each will take a turn to lead (let the children know you will tell them when to swap over): the leading partner will perform actions and their partner will follow, as if they are the mirror reflection. This can be done with or without direction, but it is a good idea to pre-prepare some suggestions that the children can choose from. These can be actions or emotions and can be used to help build connections and relationships. This activity can be a lot of fun and it also helps the children to practise recognising emotions.

# Emotion biscuits

*You will need*: plain biscuits or cupcakes or paper face shapes, and cake decorating icing or pens.

Ask the children to decorate a biscuit or cupcake (or draw on face shapes) with the different feelings they experience because their special person died. Ask them to choose three emotions and to put them on the biscuit or cupcake. Children could then share a time that they experienced the emotions with the group, but they do not have to do this if they prefer not to.

For example, 'I feel sad when I remember my Dad ... happy when I have a good memory of him ... and I feel lonely that he is not here'.

> In the group I am with other kids who understand a bit, I can talk and they get it.
> 11-year-old girl whose Dad passed away

# 12. Additional support

## Counselling

Many children navigate loss with the support of their family, friends, school staff and others around them. Sometimes children require further support, and this is when counselling may be appropriate.

It is important for school, home and other agencies to communicate concerns to one another, and to consider whether they feel the child is struggling with any of the following over a prolonged period of time:

- Aggression.
- Stomach aches, headaches and other physical symptoms.
- Difficulties sleeping, maybe with getting to sleep, nightmares or night terrors.
- Issues with eating, maybe with eating too much or too little, or a combination of the two.
- Becoming withdrawn socially and isolating themselves.
- Difficulties in school or difficulties concentrating and retaining information.
- Feelings of guilt.
- Marked changes in behaviour.
- Self-destructive or risk-taking behaviours, maybe talk of self-harm or suicide.
- Difficulties talking about their feelings.

Consider onward referrals when they look as though they might be needed and know your next step to take using the referral system so that you can ensure the children receive greater in-depth one-to-one support when necessary. Don't hesitate to seek further support for children: be assured that you know them best, and therefore you are the best people to identify any long-term difficulties that they need more specific support with.

Bereavement counsellors are specifically trained to support children with their grief.

> I just wanted to scream and tell everyone to shut up and go away before I went to talk to a counsellor. But now I know that I don't feel so angry when I talk about my brother.
> 10-year-old boy whose younger brother passed away

# Self-care for parents or family members

Remember that supporting anyone through bereavement is difficult; supporting children can often be even harder, particularly if you are bereaved too.

Bereavement can often leave us feeling powerless because we can't fix it or make things better, and, let's face it, when it comes to our kids, we want to take their pain away and make everything better.

The most important thing you can do is to reach out for support. For you to be able to support your child, you need to consider your own needs too. If you need help, ask for it. This is also a great example to set for your children.

Be kind to yourself and how you are feeling, you are grieving too, as well as supporting a child, and this is an extremely hard place to be.

Children need to feel a connection to the person who died, as well as a connection to 'safe' adults and family around them. It is OK for other family members to step in and help provide this care if your own grief feels overwhelming.

Remember you don't have to hide your grief. Seeing their family grieve can let children know that their feelings are valid and OK. They need to see that their adults are still able to cope and look after them, even though they are grieving too.

This book is all about helping children to express their thoughts and emotions. Take note from your children, express your emotions, whether that's with friends, family, a counsellor, or screaming at the top of your lungs on a mountainside, it does not matter – only that you let it out.

What can you take from this book and from the list on p. 9 to put in your own first aid kit? Children learn from us, and the best way we can teach them to look after themselves emotionally, physically and spiritually, is by showing them and involving them, not just by telling them.

Tell me and I'll forget
Show me and I may remember
Involve me and I'll understand.
– Chinese proverb

# Self-care for professionals

When we work with bereaved children and families we bring along our own experiences and feelings of loss. Supporting a child or family who are grieving can result in professionals feeling emotionally impacted too.

It is important to accept that supporting children emotionally is likely to impact upon you emotionally. Accept your own need for emotional and practical support and ensure that you take responsibility by asking for what you need.

If the situation has any similarities to your own life, it may bring back unresolved issues. The very fact that the situation involves children, the most vulnerable humans, can add to the emotional impact on professionals.

There is no way that you can effectively support others emotionally if your own emotional needs are not being met – and that is a fact, ladies and gentlemen!

Ironically, self-care is often forgotten by people who support others in need. We can often act as if our own needs don't exist, as if we can cope with anything, as if we don't need the same level of support as others do. Some of us even think we are indestructible (*guilty!*).

This is not the case. Your needs do matter, they are valid and you will burn out if you don't look after yourself – true story.

Use your network of friends and colleagues for support; they may be the best placed to understand how you are feeling. You could also consider setting up a peer support group with others in similar roles.

The well-known aviation phrase 'fit your own oxygen mask before you help others' is so relevant and true. Taking care of *you* is not selfish, it's not a waste of time, and it's not negotiable.

It is not what you do that matters, just that you do things for you, things that make you happy, that give you peace and, most importantly, that you keep doing them.

Children learn through experience and from what they see. Modelling self-care can be extremely powerful for a child to witness. On the following pages are some suggestions for self-care, like the child's first aid kit, but for adults. Spend some time considering what you might put in your own kit.

A work–life balance can sound like an impossible dream, but if you can incorporate some of the suggestions in this book into your day, you are already on your way to a healthier way of being.

# Self-care suggestions

Please note, there is absolutely no judgement here, or expectations for you to suddenly become your own self-help guru. This self-care business that I keep talking about may be alien to you, so look through the list at your leisure, and choose one or two ideas to add into your week. Feel free to add your own suggestions. (May I also point out that by reading this list you are already starting to take care of yourself – winning!)

*Smile, laugh, have fun* – Doing this releases endorphins, the body's feel-good chemical. Find your tribe. Spend time with family, friends and colleagues who make you feel good, lift you up, make you smile, and support your goals.

*An attitude of gratitude* – Feeling thankful for all the good things in your life and focusing on the things that we are thankful for can change our mood and, over time, our brains too.

*Relax* – Have a bath, pamper yourself, read, do some yoga or breathing exercises. They can all help you to relax and unwind.

*Physical activity* – Whatever gets your heart rate up a little and makes you breathe a little faster will help to release levels of the stress hormone cortisol and increase endorphins.

*Get outdoors* – Being outside, breathing in some fresh air and connecting with nature can be very beneficial. It can help you to think more clearly, get some vitamin D into your body and feel refreshed and grounded.

*Sleep* – Consider how much sleep you are getting, take an honest look at your evening routines. Sleep helps us to repair, rest and recuperate.

*Eating right (and regularly) and drinking water* – These things can all help to keep our mood stable and ensure we have enough energy. Water is needed for hydration of all the cells in the body.

*Take up a new hobby* – Whatever it is, get out there and do it. Feel good, find your passion and do something you love. Hobbies can help people to have a more positive work–life balance.

*Get creative* – Art, acting, singing or dancing can all help you to express yourself and how you are feeling.

*Social media* – Studies have shown the negative impact that social media can have on our mood, mental health and self-esteem. Consider how much time this takes up and how it impacts your mood.

*Be kind to yourself* – Notice how you talk to yourself, try to add some more positives into that dialogue. Treat yourself like you would treat the child you are supporting, with love and compassion. Please remember, we are all doing the best we can, with the resources we have available at the time in any given situation. I am sure you are doing your absolute best.

Where there is love there is no darkness.
Burundian proverb

# Useful organisations

There are many organisations that offer further support and guidance on bereavement, including:

Winston's Wish
www.winstonswish.org
0808 802 0021

Cruse Bereavement Care
www.cruse.org.uk
0808 808 1677

Child Bereavement UK
www.childbereavementuk.org
0800 02 888 40

Grief Encounter
www.griefencounter.org.uk
020 8371 8455

Childhood Bereavement Network
www.childhoodbereavementnetwork.org.uk
020 7843 6309